Happy Homeowner

7 Simple Secrets to Dreams That Last a Lifetime, Or Two

Jim Rollo

Happy Homeowner

Independently Published

Copyright © 2018, Jim Rollo

Published in the United States of America

180503-01085-3

ISBN-13: 978-1790715947

Here's What's Inside...

Dedication to Our Parents

This book is dedicated to our parents. Today, more than 20 years after our father passed away from colon cancer, our mother is still able to keep the home we grew up in. It is clear to see the wisdom of decisions made over the years and how those decisions continue to make a difference in our mother's life. By contrast, there are countless examples of surviving spouses who find themselves in serious predicaments. There is only a slight difference between surviving spouses who can keep their dream alive for two lifetimes and those who must forfeit their dream. As every day passes, it is clear that our parents knew the secrets of dreams that last a lifetime. In the case of our parents, their dream has lasted for two lifetimes.

A Noble Calling

Security and peace of mind
Are what we help our clients find

To know that when they leave this earth
They'll leave behind something of worth

A legacy for those still here
So they won't have to live in fear

To wonder if they'll keep their home
They want to stay there 'til they're grown

We advocate for hearts and feet
Who run, their mom or dad to greet

When they come home from a long day
And tuck them in then kneel and pray

For little ones we advocate
They hope we won't procrastinate

To counsel parents to insure
Their income so they'll be secure

We advocate for widows, too
Their income may depend on you

We can provide a guarantee
An income there will always be

Protecting those you leave behind
Will give you total peace of mind

So, talk to us and make it fast
We can make your income last

By Jim Rollo
March 16, 2014

I was inspired to write this poem following a Saturday
morning appointment with a young family. As their children
played together in my office, the parents and I put their
income protection plan in place. The children were depending
on me to provide wise counsel to their parents. "For little
ones we advocate"

Introduction

Happy Homeowner!

We all have experiences in life that leave a lasting impression on us. In the course of our work, we observe customers, and close family members, in the midst of "consequences." Those consequences leave a lasting impression on us. The word "consequences" is often used with a negative connotation, but it also has a positive connotation. Working with thousands of homeowners, our team of licensed insurance professionals has the opportunity to observe outcomes, both desirable and undesirable. The most impactful experiences that drive our passion to help people stay in their homes are the times we sit across the table from a customer in a moment of need. When we have worked together in advance to implement the "7 Secrets," there is a very high likelihood the customer will experience positive consequences. We are passionate about planning in a way that creates positive consequences for our customers. Customers hire us to help them create good consequences.

When we sit together with someone who is struggling to survive because of decisions made or postponed, it renews our passion to share the 7 Secrets. It is especially painful for us if the person is dealing with not so good consequences that are the result of decisions made by someone else. The decisions we make to prepare (or not) for what we call "The Storms of Life" often have serious consequences which impact our families. Customers hire us to help them make better decisions, resulting in better outcomes.

In our experience, this journey of lifetime home ownership is mostly about creating positive consequences for women. In the title of this book, the phrase "a lifetime...or two" refers to the cases when a surviving spouse, like my mother, is suddenly the person keeping the dream of homeownership alive. Statistically speaking, this surviving spouse will be a woman who has a dream of preserving homeownership for the rest of her life. Customers hire us to help them keep the dream alive for a lifetime...or two.

One of my goals in life is to accumulate passion. The passion for helping people stay in their homes is increasing as we work with thousands of Happy Homeowners.

It is my sincere desire, and the desire of our entire team, that the simple secrets will make your dreams last a lifetime...or two. They are simple secrets.

We hope this book inspires you to take action. Learn the simple secrets and apply them. Make sure you have taken the necessary steps so that your dreams will last a lifetime...or two.

To becoming a happy homeowner!

Enjoy the book!

Jim

The Dream of Homeownership!

Are you dreaming of your first home? A larger home? A smaller home? A vacation home? Are you in your golden years, saying "I (or we) want to stay in this home forever?"

Let's start where you are and imagine how, in a perfect world, your dream of homeownership would unfold over your lifetime. Imagine your story being told in this book. You have completed the journey of life as a Happy Homeowner. How would you like your story to read?

In a perfect world, there would be no surprises during life's journey, no storms of life appearing out of nowhere to derail our dreams. Imagine if you could install a special "Weather App" on your smartphone. This special "Weather App" would alert you to the storms of life which appear out of nowhere. What are the storms the app could alert you to? What are the "secret storms" that have the potential to derail your lifetime dream of home ownership? In the absence of this "Weather App," how can you know what these "secret storms" are? How can you "Weatherproof Your Dreams for the Storms of Life?" How can you achieve the peace of mind that comes with knowing your dreams will be fulfilled even if storms appear along the way?

This book is written to help you be prepared for the storms of life.

We talk about a time of life called the empty nest stage. It seems like we all have this tendency, some more than others, for nesting. We all like to have a place to lay our heads. We all like to have a place we can call home. We have an emotional attachment to the dream of homeownership. It's not only a place we call home and a place we put down roots, it can also be a symbol of accomplishment. We may think, "Through hard work and sacrifice we've been able to achieve our dream of home ownership". It's part of the fabric of our culture in the United States, and in other parts of the world as well. To say, "We've accomplished something important. No matter what else happens in our lives, we know we have a place to call home." It's a significant achievement and should not be overlooked.

Let's stop for a minute and think about the word "home". What emotions does that word bring up for you? Our home is a place of refuge and security, a place we always love to return to. Think back to your childhood and memories of the home you grew up in. Are there special childhood memories connected to the home you grew up in? Think about visiting your grandparents and spending time in their homes. I can remember my grandfather's home and have very fond memories of time spent with him. To this day, when I drive by the home that my grandfather owned the memories come flooding back to my mind. These memories of my grandfather are attached to time I spent with him at his home. There's a connection emotionally we all have with the home we grew up in, or the homes of aunts, uncles, neighbors or grandparents. There's an emotional connection that is tied to significant memories for most of us. We all like to build memories. Many of those memories are built around our homes. It's our wish that everyone has a chance to raise their families and build lasting memories in a home that will last a lifetime...or two.

The 7 Secrets to Dreams That Last a Lifetime, Or Two

"The 7 Secrets to Dreams That Last a Lifetime, Or Two" came to me through experience working with thousands of homeowners. We work with homeowners of every age. We serve customers in their early 20s buying their first home. We serve customers in their 90s who have owned their homes for 50+ years, and everyone in between. Working with people of all ages has helped us develop a broad perspective. Every day we see customers facing the "storms of life", those unexpected events that occur in all of our lives. When storms come up, our preparation and what we like to call our "weatherproofing" is put to the test. In the face of the storms of life, there is one common desire we have seen among our customers. All of our customers want to preserve their dream of home ownership. They want to come through the storms of life and know their home is secure.

When the storms of life come, suddenly we find ourselves face to face with consequences. The consequences we face are most likely a result of the decisions we have made. We are working with people in every age group and we witness close up the consequences of decisions they've made. What do you think when you hear the word "consequences"? The word "consequences" may bring up a negative feeling. You may think, "Oh no, what's going to happen now if there are consequences?" For most of us, that word has a negative connotation. In fact, "consequences" has both positive and negative connotations. In our work, we see that good decisions have good consequences, and not-so-good decisions have not-so-good consequences.

We've had the benefit of assisting thousands of people, across all age groups, as they face the storms of life. We see how decisions they've made previously have resulted in certain outcomes. In our work, we are in a unique position to observe positive consequences and not so positive consequences. We have witnessed the dream of home ownership live on after the storms of life, and we have witnessed the dream of home ownership end abruptly.

Walking with our customers through the storms of life builds a steady accumulation of wisdom. Learning from decisions made by our customers and seeing the consequences of those decisions renews our passion to accumulate wisdom, and to dispense that wisdom. Our desire to share what we have learned has led to what we call the 7 Simple Secrets. The 7 Simple Secrets are the things we have observed which will help you better prepare and weatherproof your dreams.

You may be wondering "Why are they called secrets?" "Why aren't these simple secrets widely known?" Too often the knowledge can get lost in the shuffle. When going through the process of buying a home, people are in a whirlwind of real estate agents, mortgages, documents, home inspections, closing attorneys, and appraisers. Once the closing is over, the move in date is set and then life happens. Little time is available for discussions about how to preserve the dream of home ownership for a lifetime...or two.

They are secrets in the sense that they're often overlooked. They're missing from the process. It's not because anyone is deliberately trying to conceal them.

Sharing this accumulated wisdom is what we do every day. Now, this book will help us get the word out to more people who can benefit from the 7 Simple Secrets.

Simple Secret #1: Happy Homeowners Weatherproof Their Home's Value

The first simple secret is to weatherproof the value of your home. "What is the value of your home?" Depending on who you ask, the value of your home can vary drastically. Real Estate Appraisers, Tax Assessors, and Real Estate Agents will most likely provide you with different valuations for your home. As market conditions vary, the valuations of your home can move up or down. To weatherproof your home's value, the most important number to know is the replacement cost of your home. What would the cost be to rebuild your home in the event of a catastrophe? The replacement value of your home is the number that matters most if an unforeseen event occurs. Our goal is to preserve your dream of home ownership. Replacement value is the number that's going to preserve your dream.

Knowing the replacement cost of your home can be achieved by working with a licensed insurance professional. After working with thousands of families over the years, it is rare to find a homeowner who has worked with an insurance professional to calculate the replacement cost of their home. Your home may be the most expensive purchase you will ever make. Leaving the replacement cost valuation to chance is risky business.

If you have not done so already, request a copy of the replacement cost estimate from your insurance professional. If you are working with a knowledgeable insurance professional, you can obtain a copy of the replacement cost estimate for your home. Ask how the estimated replacement cost was calculated. The insurance professional you're working with can tell you that. Request an appointment to walk through the replacement cost calculation with your insurance professional. In all likelihood, there is a computer program used to calculate the replacement cost. You can walk through the process to be sure the inputs to the calculator are accurate, resulting in a precise replacement cost estimate.

Following are some stories of experiences we have walked through with our customers. These are moments of truth when our weatherproofing was put to the test.

Here's a story about John and Cindy. It was early afternoon on a beautiful fall day in upstate New York. Cindy went shopping with friends and John was busy winterizing the swimming pool. After finishing the work with the wet vacuum around the pool, John went into the house to take a nap. Shortly after falling asleep, John awoke to the sound of the family dog barking. John immediately realized why the dog was barking. The whole back of the home was engulfed in flames. John ran outside and called 911 on his cell phone. The fire company arrived quickly, but the home was a total loss. The family dog saved John's life. Fortunately, John and Cindy had replacement coverage for their home and contents so the rebuilding process could begin right away.

Another customer story involves one of the most common questions people ask us, "What if my neighbor's tree falls on my house?"

Beth works as a volunteer at a local not-for-profit. One afternoon, around 4PM Beth arrived home from her volunteer work to find that a large tree had fallen from her neighbor's property on to her house. The tree damaged the roof and tore some of the siding off the house. As the tree fell it also took down the electrical wires, the phone wires, and the TV cable. Beth came into our office upset and worried about what had happened.

Within 30 minutes, we had a tree service at her home removing the tree from her roof. The next morning, we arranged for contractors to start working on restoring the electrical service and replacement of the roof. We replaced the vinyl siding on the entire house because we couldn't find a match for the siding. Beth had good coverage. She also knew that she could come to us, and we could help her get back on her feet with her house as quickly as possible.

During our fact finding interviews with home owners we always have a conversation about detached structures. Here's a story about one of our customers who came into our office worried about coverage for his detached structure. The reason for his concern was due to an unfortunate event. Mike is a foreman for a local construction company. One morning Mike came into our office looking quite concerned and a bit panicked. He asked if we could review his coverage for the large detached garage and workshop at his home. We reviewed the coverage and confirmed that when we had originally insured Mike's home we recommended additional coverage for his garage and workshop. So, Mike was covered.

Mike looked relieved, knowing that he was covered and then proceeded to explain the reason for his concern. Mike had just spent time in North Carolina at his son's home. Mike helped build a large detached garage and workshop for his son. When Mike came back home to New York, he received a call from his son to tell him that the newly built garage and workshop had burned to the ground. Unfortunately, Mike's son had not contacted his insurance professional to request additional detached structure coverage. The cost to rebuild the structure exceeded the standard coverage that is provided by the homeowner policy.

The moral of that story is we're all going to beautify our homes to some degree. Make sure you notify your insurance carrier before you do something like build a garage, build a barn, put an addition on, or remodel your house. It's better to be safe than sorry. Call your insurance professional and say, "I am planning to do the following improvements. Maybe it's a good idea to go back through the replacement cost estimate and update it so that the coverage is going to be adequate to protect our home." This can save you thousands of dollars.

Having replacement cost coverage does not mean you are obligated to rebuild the home. Our recent experience with one of our customers illustrates this. Mary, a 70-year-old widow experienced a total loss of her home. Her home burned to the ground and was literally a pile of ashes. All of Mary's personal property was also destroyed in the fire. There was nothing left. Mary decided she didn't want to rebuild. She said to me, "I'm 70 years old and I have Multiple Sclerosis. I'm going to go live with my daughter." We gave Mary a check for the actual cash value of her home and her contents. She could have used the available coverage to replace the home, but she decided to opt out and take the actual cash value instead. She was very happy with the outcome.

One scenario we often encounter today is a customer operating a business at home. What is considered a business at home can include paid activities such as speech therapy, music lessons or an art studio, just to name a few. In one case, we read about a homeowner who was operating an art studio from home. An area of the home was set aside for the art studio. A fire occurred at the home which originated in the art studio. The homeowner policy did not have a business insurance rider and the claim was not covered.

Weatherproofing your home's value involves having a conversation with your insurance professional to be sure all your potential risks are understood. You can decide to acquire the appropriate protection, or not. The choice is yours.

When we get to Simple Secret #4 we will talk more about how operating a business from home presents a risk worth covering.

We often receive inquiries regarding insurance to cover flooding. What is a flood? That is an important question. A flood is two or more adjoining properties, one of which is yours, temporarily inundated with water. Here's an example. Your neighbor has an above-ground swimming pool. That above-ground swimming pool collapses and floods your property and your neighbor's property and fills your basement with water. The only thing that will cover that scenario is flood insurance. If your neighbor's pool bursts and the water fills up your house, flood insurance is what will cover that. That's an example of what constitutes a flood.

We had flooding here in Upstate New York in 2006 and in 2011. Our area made national news because of historic flood waters rising to damage thousands of properties. We have many flood insurance policies in force. We had many customers with claims. We personally went out with the claims adjusters to visit the flood damaged homes of our policyholders. When you acquire coverage to protect your home, what are you purchasing? You're purchasing a promise. In our business, we're selling a promise. What is that promise? That promise is if something happens, we're going to be there. When the floods happened, why did we go out with the claims adjusters? We wanted to be sure that our policyholders were being paid. It was a good opportunity to hug them, reassure them, and then follow up to get their claims paid quickly. It's what we call a moment of truth. When a claim occurs, is your insurance professional running toward you and toward the problem or going in the other direction? To us, that's the real value that we provide. When the moment of truth comes, that's when you need us the most.

Hurricane Sandy hit the east coast a few years ago. Thousands of homes were damaged or destroyed completely. Local or national catastrophes like Hurricane Sandy can result in temporary increases in the cost of building materials. A significant hurricane, or multiple hurricanes occurring back to back, can increase the cost of building materials around the country. Suddenly, the cost to rebuild your house can increase because of temporary, or perhaps permanent inflation in the cost of building materials.

Having replacement value coverage on your home with an inflation rider provides a certain amount of protection against gradual increases in the replacement cost of your home.

Some insurance companies give you an extra amount above the replacement cost. This extra coverage provides a cushion in the event of any increases in the cost of materials.

A few other cases we see involve detached structures including "off premises structures" and detached garage apartments. Let's start with off premises structures. Sometimes, people have a barn or a garage at another property they own. There's no dwelling on the property, only a barn. We can add the off premises structure to your homeowner policy. We're covering that structure for replacement value, and we're covering liability at that location.

Let's say you have a detached garage behind your home. There is an apartment on the second floor of the garage. You are the owner of the detached garage with the second floor apartment, but you are not the occupant of the apartment. As a non-owner occupied dwelling the garage apartment requires special coverage for a rental property. Even if your mother-in-law is living there, it is still considered a non-owner occupied dwelling. In the absence of proper coverage for a non-owner occupied dwelling, a claim could be denied.

If you had a serious claim at your home, you might ask yourself, "Well, where am I going to live?" There's coverage that's called "loss of use," which will provide the value of additional living expenses you incur while your home is being restored. That's an important part of weatherproofing the value of your home.

We do not have the time or space in this book to cover every possible set of circumstances. The final summary of Simple Secret #1 is to work with an insurance professional to determine a replacement cost for your home and any other structures. Make sure you get a copy of the replacement cost estimate, so you know what it is.

When we work with our customers, we conduct an in depth interview to learn details of each person's situation. Based on our findings, we recommend customized protection.

Simple Secret #2: Happy Homeowners Weatherproof Their Treasure

Simple Secret #2 weatherproofing your treasure is about knowing the limitations of your homeowner policy to replace your personal property. You may have certain high value items we refer to as "Ice, Bling and Other Things". Examples of valuables that deserve special attention because of limited coverage on a homeowner policy include jewelry, watches, and coin collections. Some of these special treasures have sentimental value. These deserve special attention because (A), they have limited coverage on a homeowner policy; (B), they have limited coverage as far as what kinds of events are covered.

A good example of this is an engagement ring. Let's say there is a single diamond in the engagement ring, or the ring may have multiple diamonds. Suddenly, you notice one of the stones is missing. The stone mysteriously disappeared. Our customer says "I don't know what happened. I looked at my ring and the stone was missing. It must have fallen out of the setting." That is an example of mysterious disappearance which is not covered on a homeowner's policy. A special policy, called "personal articles," covers items of exceptional value and includes coverage for mysterious disappearance.

Other valuables with limited coverage on a homeowner policy include coin collections, musical instruments, firearms, stamp collections, etc... Be sure to discuss details of valuable items you own with your insurance professional.

Another thing to consider in order to properly Weatherproof Your Treasure is what we refer to as "Modern Family Matters". Family, friend and significant other living arrangements matter and should be discussed in detail so your insurance professional can make recommendations.

Let's talk about relatives first. Here's a scenario of a real case that happened. Mom and dad own a home, they have a home insurance policy and they are each named as insured on the policy. Their daughter, son-in-law and their three grandchildren live with them in the residence. They experience a fire and the home sustains substantial damage. The personal property of mom and dad is damaged and destroyed. The personal property of the daughter, son-in-law, and grandchildren is also lost in the fire.

The personal property of the daughter, son-in-law and grandchildren is covered, provided the policy limits are adequate. The check for the personal property of resident relatives is made payable to the named insured on the policy. Mom and dad are each the named insured, so the check is made payable to them. The parents now must decide how much they are going to give to the daughter, son-in-law, and the grandchildren for their personal property.

That can create a family issue. A better solution in this situation is for the daughter and son-in-law to have their own renter's insurance policy to cover their personal property. A single renter's policy naming the daughter and son-in-law as named insured would provide payment directly to them for their contents. They're not at the mercy of Mom and Dad or negotiating with Mom and Dad to try to get paid for their property. You might say, "Well, Mom and Dad aren't charging me rent." Renter's insurance covers personal property even if you don't "pay rent". A renter's policy covers your property and makes you first in line to be paid in the event of a claim. As the named insured, your belongings are protected.

What about non-related household members? This is very common today. One of the household members is purchasing the home. The other person, such as a significant other or life partner, is sharing the household expenses. However, this person is not on the mortgage, the deed or the insurance policy for the home.

It's critical that the significant other, a non-related household member, has coverage for their contents. In the previous case, the property of the daughter, son-in-law, and grandchildren was covered because they are resident relatives. In this case, the non-related household member doesn't have property coverage at all. In the absence of a renter's policy for a significant other, they don't have any coverage for their contents. Again, purchasing renter's insurance does not require the insured to be paying rent. They get a policy to cover their contents. If there's a fire or any claim, a check will be issued to the named insured on the renter's policy.

Weatherproofing Your Treasure may also include what we refer to as "Toy Stories." The toys we hear stories about include things like tractors, golf cars, ATVs, boats, jet skis, and campers. We will discuss these toys again later on in Simple Secret #4. For the purposes of Weatherproofing Your Treasure, we will ask about replacing toys in the event they are damaged.

Let me share with you a story of a customer who owned a travel trailer. The travel trailer was set up in a very nice campground. Fortunately, the customer was away from the campground when a windstorm came through. The customer returned to the campground to find the windstorm had uprooted a large pine tree. The customer sent me a photo of the damage. The travel trailer had been sliced in half by the fallen tree. The 32 foot long travel trailer was split into two 16 foot sections by the downed pine tree. The customer had physical damage coverage to replace the travel trailer, which was a total loss.

With very few exceptions, toys like ATVs, boats, jet skis, campers, snowmobiles, tractors, etc....are not covered on a homeowner policy. They require a separate policy to provide coverage for them which can typically be obtained for very little money.

When it comes to weatherproofing your treasure, it's a good idea to prepare a home inventory. We provide our customers with a home inventory checklist so they can write down a list of all the contents of their house. We can upload the inventory listing on our secure drive for safekeeping. If something happens in their house and the list gets destroyed, we have it on file. We store a record of their inventory for them to refer to in the event of a claim.

Is a home inventory required in the event of a claim? No. Is it helpful? Yes. It helps you to jog your memory and to make sure that you're giving the insurance company all the details they need.

Another treasure to consider weatherproofing is your identity. Today, one of the risks we all face is identity theft. Happy homeowners make sure to weatherproof their identity. An optional coverage available on many homeowner policies today is called Identity Restoration Coverage. The coverage pays the expenses associated with restoring your identity and cleaning up credit reports. Some companies will assign a case manager to handle the restoration process for you and pay certain legal expenses associated with restoration of your identity.

Simple Secret #3:
Happy Homeowners Get Regular Oil Changes

Happy homeowners get regular oil changes. The fact that regular oil changes are essential to keep the engine in your car running is widely known. You may have been advised to change the oil every 3,000 miles, to rotate your tires and top off fluids. Most states have laws which require your car to pass an annual inspection to verify compliance with minimum standards. We must rectify any issues that may be preventing our car from passing the state inspection.

How well informed are we when it comes to regular maintenance to keep our home running? In my experience, the maintenance requirements for our home are not as widely understood as are the requirements for our cars.

The manufacturer of an automobile provides an owner's manual with the recommended service and maintenance schedule. When we purchase a home, we do not receive an owner's manual. Does it seem logical that we know more about the required maintenance for a car than we know about the required maintenance for our home? Our cars rapidly depreciate in value. Our home is purchased with the hope that it will appreciate, and it may be the largest purchase we ever make during our lifetime. Yet, we know relatively little about the required maintenance of our home. "Does that make sense?"

Our goal is to help the happy homeowners learn about maintenance and develop a plan for maintenance. We provide resources and tools to help you understand and schedule predictive and preventive maintenance so you can avoid a catastrophe. Why do we change the oil in our car? We would rather spend money to change the oil than spend money to replace the engine. The same concept applies to our home.

For example, the furnace and air conditioner in a home require regular maintenance. Minimum maintenance requirements include inspection, cleaning and filter replacements. Performing regular maintenance on your heating and air conditioning system can prevent a major catastrophe.

We provide a home appliance inventory sheet so that our customers can take inventory of their home appliances. On one sheet of paper a record can be made of the brand, the model number, the serial number, and the date installed.

Some systems in our homes have planned maintenance or a certain life expectancy. Just like some automobiles have a planned maintenance item, such as a timing belt. On certain automobiles, the owner's manual states the timing belt must be changed at 90,000 miles. If you don't replace the timing belt and the belt breaks the engine can seize. That's a bad day.

We provide our customers the tools they need to develop a preventive maintenance plan. If a hot water heater is reaching its life expectancy, is it better to replace it before it starts to leak? If you wait until it leaks, what damage will the leak cause?

We give our customers a water loss prevention checklist. We encourage them to create a schedule for preventing and checking for water leaks. One of the most common water leaks resulting in homeowner claims is a burst washing machine hose. The water loss prevention checklist recommends periodically checking washing machine hoses and replacing rubber hoses with metal braided hoses.

Another common occurrence in the northeast is a frozen water pipe which cracks or bursts. Here's an example of an experience one of our customers had with a frozen water line. We received a call from a customer telling us his waterline froze and burst on the first floor of the house. They were unable to access the main shutoff to stop the water. The customer said, "My house is filling up with water, and we can't turn it off." We were able to get the local municipality on the phone by calling their emergency number. They were able to go out and shut the waterline off at the road. Thankfully, the water stopped pouring in and filling their house with water, but not before a substantial amount of damage occurred.

It is critical to know where your water shutoffs are before a crisis occurs. It is also recommended to have a plumber install multiple shutoffs at various points so you can isolate sections of your house in the event of a leak. Think about the electrical panel in your house. The panel has breakers from which you can shut off certain parts of your house to be able to work on them. If you had to replace an outlet or do electrical work, you could shut off certain rooms. The same is true of water. It's a good idea to put shutoffs in strategic places to be able to shut off certain sections of your home. In the event of a leak, you can shut the water off only in the affected area.

We have developed a Home Owner's Manual which includes resources designed to help you create a preventive maintenance plan. When a customer purchases home insurance with one of our agencies, we prepare a customized Home Owner's Manual for the customer.

Some state governments mandate automobiles pass an annual inspection to remain in service. When it comes to annual inspection of our homes, we must hold ourselves accountable. We are responsible to see that annual inspections of our homes are performed.

We can provide you with tools and resources to be help you develop a plan for maintenance and inspections.

Simple Secret #4: Happy Homeowners Know Their Limits

Happy Homeowners Know Their Limits when it comes to liability. Your dream of home ownership can be derailed by a liability issue, even if the event did not occur at your home. For example, an automobile accident can have consequences which include making your home available as a financial resource to settle a claim.

The number one risk that most of us face relates to what we call America's new pastime. Baseball was once referred to as America's pastime. From what we see on television ads, the new pastime may be lawsuits.

Personal injury lawsuits are an epidemic in our country. All you have to do is turn on the TV for five minutes, and you can see personal injury lawyers who are flashing their phone numbers and their websites on the screen. The ads are asking about different scenarios that you might have encountered which could make you eligible to enter a lawsuit against another party and collect damages. If you suddenly find yourself on the wrong side of a personal injury lawsuit it will give you peace of mind to know you are protected.

We want to make sure you are educated about what your risks are. Think about a claim to your home, maybe a kitchen fire with a $50,000 cost to replace your kitchen. The cost to replace your kitchen is a finite number, $50,000. Even if we had to rebuild your entire home, and the replacement cost was $250,000., that's a finite number. By contrast, a personal injury claim, because somebody slips and falls at your house, is not necessarily a finite number. If someone is injured and can no longer work, a court may look at the lifetime earning potential of that person. A judge may say, "You're responsible for making that person whole because they slipped and fell at your house. The lifetime earning potential of the injured person has now been diminished or completely eliminated." The lifetime earning potential of an injured person can be a very large number. We want to make sure you understand the risk and the available options to provide coverage for such an event.

There are other liability risks which may impact your home. Some of those risks may include accidents with autos, ATVs, boats, jet skis, and snowmobiles, etc.... You may decide to forego physical damage coverage on some of the toys mentioned above. However, it is important to make a clear decision about liability protection for autos, ATVs, boats, jet skis and snowmobiles. We want to make sure you understand the risk and the available options to provide coverage for a liability claim. What can happen in an accident, and how does that relate to your home? As discussed previously, in some states a court may be able to put a lien on your home as a way to make an injured party whole. A lien could prevent you from transferring title of that home until a person who's been injured has been paid in full. That's an important factor, potentially putting your home at risk because of decisions you made about liability coverage.

A few years ago, a single dad came into our office and he purchased a personal liability umbrella policy. A few months later, his son had a car accident where he T-boned a couple in an intersection. We paid a large sum of money in that claim. If he had not purchased the umbrella policy, he would have put his personal financial resources in jeopardy.

One way to think of liability limits is to imagine them as a hurdle. Before a person can reach your personal financial resources, they must get over the hurdle. Your choice of liability limits determines the height of that hurdle. How high do you want that hurdle to be?

Typically, the annual cost for an umbrella policy is less than the cost of a one-hour consultation with an attorney you may hire to defend you. If we find ourselves on the wrong end of a personal injury lawsuit, and we're the defendant, then we want to make sure we have that coverage. Many umbrella policies include legal representation in addition to the liability coverage.

Happy homeowners know their limits, and they make decisions to choose appropriate coverage.

Simple Secret #5: Happy Homeowners Weatherproof Their Income

Happy Homeowners Weatherproof Their Income. When one of life's storms appears and puts your income at risk, how can you be sure your dream of home ownership will not be in jeopardy? Weatherproofing your income means protecting against temporary or permanent reduction of your income to keep your dream alive.

The two most common events that have the potential to put our income at risk are disability or death. One of these two risks, namely disability, is a temporary risk which we face only during our working years. In the case of death, it can be considered a lifetime risk. In almost every case, when one household member dies, household income will be reduced. This is true during a person's working years, and it is also true after retirement.

The conventional wisdom is homeowners should only protect their income if they have a mortgage. Once the mortgage is paid off, there's no longer a need for income protection.

The truth is that a reduction in household income can have consequences even after your mortgage is paid off. After your mortgage is paid off, household income is still a requirement to keep the dream of home ownership alive. The title of this book refers to dreams that last a lifetime...or two. The dream of home ownership will last a lifetime...or two as long as there is income coming into the household for a lifetime...or two. When one or more household income sources are reduced or discontinued, what will happen to your dream?

This simple secret, weatherproofing your income, may be the most misunderstood of all the simple secrets. It is misunderstood because there is a message being broadcast to all of us that is an incomplete truth. The incomplete truth being spread is that income protection, weatherproofing your income is a priority until your mortgage is paid off. The complete truth is weatherproofing your income is a lifetime necessity, because lifetime income is necessary.

How do we make sure that there's sufficient income that will last a lifetime...or two?

For a 25-year-old first time home buyer, weatherproofing income involves protection against disability and death. At a bare minimum, the requirement will be to cover the mortgage in the event that one of life's storms appears.

When a 75-year-old whose mortgage is paid off suddenly finds herself a widow, what does she need? She needs enough guaranteed lifetime income to keep her dream of homeownership alive. As soon as she becomes a widow, she faces a reduction in income. At a minimum, the total value of household social security income will be reduced. There may be other income sources that are reduced or eliminated at the death of one spouse.

So, the 25 year old first time home buyer and the 75 year old recently widowed homeowner have a common need for income to keep their dreams alive. In both cases, a storm of life can appear that puts a dent in household income, thereby jeopardizing the dream of home ownership.

If we believe income to be an essential ingredient to keep the dream of home ownership alive, and we believe the dream is a lifetime dream, then why do we listen to a message that counsels income protection only during working years, or only while we still have a mortgage?

A lifetime dream requires a lifetime of income. It is clear to see that our customer who is a newly widowed 75 year old needs a special kind of income. She needs Guaranteed Lifetime Income.

Stop right here for a moment. Let's zero in on the power of those three words combined together. Those three words create a phrase that describes one of the most powerful and desirable concepts in human history. What is that concept? That concept is "Guaranteed Lifetime Income".

We pay into a social safety net and in return receive a meaningful benefit in the form of social security income. The one thing we all like about social security is the promise that social security income is considered guaranteed lifetime income. Social security income will be reduced when one spouse passes away. However, there is a certain peace of mind in knowing that one of the social security benefits will remain intact.

From a very young age we are encouraged to save for the future. During my college years, working as a waiter in restaurants provided a source of income. One of our fellow waiters was a retiree named Joe. He enjoyed working to stay active and get out of the house. Joe would always counsel us with his words of wisdom "Save your money, it's later than you think". Joe was right!

Accumulating a valuable financial nest egg is a goal many of us share. We're saving money for the future. We may be saving money for retirement. We're accumulating money toward a future goal. At some point in life, the real value of that nest egg will not be determined by its size. The value will not be determined by how many zeroes there are in our nest egg statement. The value will be determined by the guaranteed lifetime income that nest egg can produce. How long is a lifetime? If we have guaranteed lifetime income, the answer to the question has to be "It doesn't matter how long a lifetime is, the income will still be there. Guaranteed."

In many cases, the desire will be for the nest egg to produce guaranteed lifetime income for a lifetime...or two. In other words, when one spouse passes away, the nest egg will continue to produce guaranteed lifetime income for the surviving spouse.

Is the guaranteed lifetime income generated by our nest egg a supplement to social security, or is social security a supplement to our nest egg?

One of the things we do, working with thousands of people, is to step back and learn from their circumstances. Reality can shatter our preconceived notions. The idea that income protection is a short-term issue, ending when the mortgage is paid off, has been proven wrong repeatedly. Income protection is a lifetime issue. We have witnessed divorced and widowed customers struggle financially, and in some cases forfeit their dream of home ownership. We have also seen people who've made good choices experience good outcomes and good consequences.

One example would be my parents. Today, more than 20 years after my father passed away, my mother is still living in the home. Her dream is to stay in the home. She will be able to stay in the home because of good choices that they made.

When a retiree has suddenly been confronted with a reduced household income, it is a shock. Many times, they come to us looking for solutions.

If we previously worked together on simple secret number five, and we've acted to ensure the customer has guaranteed lifetime income, the impact of a significant life change can be minimized or overcome completely.

During working years, we describe weatherproofing income against the storm of disability by using the acronym H.U.G. The acronym means Housing, Utilities and Groceries. We counsel customers to "HUG your family". At a minimum, cover: Housing, Utilities, and Groceries. If you have those things, and you're unable to work temporarily due to a disability, you at least have the basics covered.

Weatherproofing income against the storms of life also includes coverage for a stay-at-home parent who passes away prematurely. It is a pleasure to sit with customers who work as stay-at-home spouses and help calculate the financial value they bring to the family. They enjoy seeing that number. They enjoy sharing that number with their spouse. It reaffirms their value and their self-esteem.

Allow me to share some stories. These stories illustrate how we have helped customers weatherproof their income.

John and Elizabeth are first time home buyers, both are 30 years old and healthy. John works at a university and Elizabeth stays home with their new baby. When we sat together to discuss plans to weatherproof his income against the storms of life, John made a decision to move forward and put an income protection plan in place. A few months later, John contacted me to say he'd been diagnosed with a brain tumor. Fortunately, we were able to replace his income during his time of disability. We weatherproofed his income, and he was a happy homeowner. The money we were providing during John's disability was used to pay their mortgage. John and Elizabeth are still happy homeowners because they chose to move ahead with the decision to weatherproof his income.

Bill, a 40-year-old homeowner and single dad, came in to meet with me. Bill, who was raising his 10 year old son, shared with me how he spent time with his son by coaching his sports teams. We talked about life insurance. Bill decided to purchase a life insurance policy. Twenty-one months later, it was a shock to read Bill's obituary in the newspaper. While getting dressed to go to work he dropped dead of a heart attack. Bill had made the decision to weatherproof his income. Bill is gone, but he left something valuable for his son.

Even beyond the grave, dad has left a legacy of love for his son. He weatherproofed his income. Bill's son still lives in the same house. He's being cared for by a family member, and still lives in his dad's house. Bill's son wasn't uprooted because we did the right work and weatherproofed his dad's income. Even though Bill isn't here, we could say he is still a happy homeowner because he weatherproofed his income. His son is enjoying the consequences of Bill's good choice.

Bill's family is administering the money for the benefit of his son. When the time comes, Bill's son will have his needs met for his first car, college education and his first home. Pretty good consequences after the storm of life.

It would be wonderful if all the situations we experience with our customers were happily ever after stories. Unfortunately, there are many stories of families faced with storms of life and there is no protection in place. Friends and family gather to put on spaghetti dinners or online fund raisers to help overcome the aftermath of an unforeseen storm.

We continue to share the message that income is a lifetime necessity to keep the dream alive. Income that lasts a lifetime, or two...requires weatherproofing for a lifetime...or two.

Simple Secret #6:
Happy Homeowners Keep Costs Down

Happy homeowners keep costs down by doing a couple of simple things. First, many insurance companies offer what's known in insurance vernacular as a "multi-line discount." Happy homeowners ask, "Does the insurance company I'm working with offer a multi-line discount? If I insure my auto and my home, will the cost of my home insurance go down? Will the cost of my auto insurance go down? If I purchase the personal liability umbrella (which we talked about in simple secret number four), will that add another discount?"

Multiple line discounts are one of the ways to keep costs down. If you combine your policies with one carrier, many companies give you an incentive in the form of a discount. That helps you keep costs down.

Many insurance companies reward loyalty by providing additional discounts. This may help you keep costs down. Staying with the same insurance company for a long time, may bring rewards in the form of lower premiums. Another discount may be available for claim-free years that you've been insured with that company. If you're insured with a company, and you stay claim-free, what are the prospects of seeing your premiums go down over time?

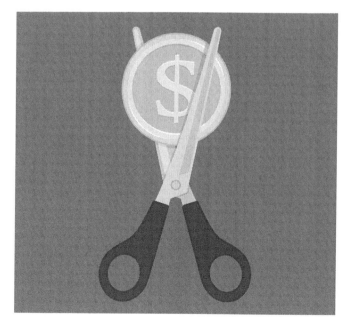

Another thing that can provide an opportunity to keep costs down is a home security system. If you have a home security system that reports into central monitoring, chances are you're going to be eligible for a discount. Will that discount pay for the home security system? Probably not, but it will provide a discount. Many times, people who have a home security system don't tell their insurance company, and they're forfeiting the discount without knowing it. We want to make sure you're knowledgeable and aware of available discounts and a home security system discount is one of them.

Another great way to keep costs down on the homeowner's insurance is managing deductibles. We call this having skin in the game. When we, as the homeowner, have skin in the game by saying, "I'll select a higher deductible. By selecting that higher deductible, I will be rewarded in the form of lower insurance premiums on my home."

Typically, you might think about having a deductible that's 1% of the replacement cost. Your home has a $300,000 replacement value. Your deductible is 1% of replacement value. That's a $3,000 deductible. Let's look at the payback. "Well if we have a $1,000 deductible versus a $3,000 deductible, and you save $200 per year, how many years will it take for us to recover that difference? For how many years must we go without a claim before we recover that difference?" The answer in this case is to divide the deductible difference by the difference in annual premiums. $2,000 / $200 = 10 years. Most people in their lifetime never have a homeowner claim. The odds are that selecting a higher deductible will help you keep costs down.

By selecting a lower deductible, you're choosing to give more money to the insurance company because you are transferring more risk to them.

Almost 100% of the homeowner policies that we write have higher deductibles. We present our customers the choice of keeping their money or giving their money to the insurance company. Almost 100% of the people choose to keep their money. They're rewarded with a lower premium in exchange for a higher deductible. If a claim happens, they have a higher deductible. If a claim never happens, the deductible is irrelevant. We counsel customers to keep their money and keep costs down.

You may be tempted to keep your costs down by cutting coverage. Cutting your coverage to keep costs down is a last resort. You'll be better off combining policies and increasing your deductibles to lower your premiums and keep cost down. That's how happy homeowners keep costs down.

Simple Secret #7: Happy Homeowners Have a Plan

When we say Happy Homeowners Have a Plan, we are referring to an exit plan. What will happen to your home when you turn off the lights for the last time? What do you want to see happen? Do you want to leave that to chance? Do you want to leave that to a probate court? Do you want to run the risk of a family feud upon your departure from this life, or do you want to have a plan?

There are simple steps you can take to develop a plan. You can develop a plan that will outlive you. That's the goal; create a plan that outlives you. By making a few choices in advance, you can spare your loved ones from unnecessary time and expense after your departure.

We recommend meeting with a member of the legal profession to help prepare your plan. The do it yourself option comes with certain risks that your plan will not be carried out. Your plan may require maintenance over time, so it is advisable to periodically review your plan with a member of the legal profession to be sure it is still relevant and up to date.

Here are some of the questions to think about:

Do you have will?

Do you have a living will?

Do you have a durable power of attorney?

Have you updated beneficiary designations?

Do you have P.O.D. (payable on death) beneficiaries on bank accounts?

More than once a customer has said to me "I don't need to do estate planning because I don't have an estate. That's for rich people."

The fact is, we all need a plan. The plan we each develop is customized to achieve our own personal goals. Do you have dreams that extend beyond your lifetime? Proper planning can ensure that your dreams last a lifetime...or two... and beyond.

"A good person leaves an inheritance for their children's children..." Proverbs 13:22

Happy Homeowners Have a Plan.

Your 7 Simple Secrets Peace of Mind Scorecard

We have developed a special tool, The Happy Homeowner Scorecard, to help determine how your current plan measures up against the 7 Simple Secrets. Every time we meet with a Happy Homeowner to improve their 7 Simple Secrets Scorecard, we make a promise. Every day, we step in on behalf of Happy Homeowners to keep those promises. Storms of life come in like a force of nature. We are a force of nature, too. We are a very strong weatherproofing powerhouse with the most trusted and respected name in the industry. Trust and respect are earned through promises made and promises kept. We are promise keepers. That's what we do. That's who we are. We deliver when the storms of life appear.

Now that you know all 7 Simple Secrets, contact us so we can write your story. When you contact us, we have an initial interview. We're going to walk you through the 7 secrets and make sure you are protected. We will ask you questions designed to help you make good choices. You will make educated choices. We want you to be able to make choices consistent with the outcomes you want, consistent with the consequences you want.

We will ask questions about your home. We will learn about the details of your home and the plans you have to improve your home. We will calculate the replacement cost of your home and provide you with a copy of the replacement cost estimate.

We will ask you things like, "Do you have a business in your home? Are you planning significant improvements? If yes, let's go through what they are, so we can make sure you have the right coverage for that."

We will learn about any special treasure that you might have. What are the items you own that are exceptionally valuable to you? We'll show you what your options are to weatherproof your treasure.

We will provide you with tools to create a plan for maintenance of your home.

We will discuss your limits with you. We will help you understand your limits and your risks.

We will help you understand choices regarding protection of your income.

We will show you options to help keep your costs down.

We will provide you with resources to help you create a plan that will outlive you.

You may not have realized it while reading the book, but we have actually given you a "Bonus Secret".

The Bonus Secret is "Happy Homeowners Have Guaranteed Income for a Lifetime...Or Two".

Income is like the magic glue that holds all the other secrets together. Guaranteed Lifetime Income keeps the dream alive. Guaranteed.

To get started, email me at
Jim@happyhomeownerbook.com

Or call me at **(607) 242-2086**

My website **www.happyhomeownerbook.com**

Together, Let's Build Your Better Future For A Lifetime...Or Two.

Building Dreams That Last a Lifetime...Or Two, Is a Journey All Homeowners Are On

Are you dreaming of your first home? A larger home? A smaller home? A vacation home? Are you relocating? Are you in your golden years? How well prepared are you and your loved ones for the unexpected events that suddenly appear along the way?

That's where we come in. We help people just like you weatherproof their dreams for the storms of life. By applying the seven simple secrets, we build an unshakable foundation to preserve your dreams for a lifetime...or two.

Step 1: Email me at **Jim@happyhomeownerbook.com** for a copy of the Happy Homeowner Scorecard. Your scorecard will help you determine how your current plans measure up. You will gain clarity in your thinking and planning for a better future. If there were gaps in your weatherproofing, when would you want to know?

Step 2: We create an action plan to help you get from where you are now to where you want to be. What's it going to take to get there? We help you do that.

Step 3: We work with you to prioritize the timing of implementing your plan to keep your homeownership dream alive for a lifetime...or two.

Many people learn the simple secrets through the school of hard knocks. They only find out they aren't protected by trial and error, as they confront the storms of life. That's when the question comes up "Why didn't anyone tell me?" None of us are exempt.

Having learned the simple secrets, you are now in a position to anticipate the storms of life. You can weatherproof your dreams for the storms of life. You can join the ranks of the happy homeowners, and know that your dreams can last a lifetime...or two.

Send me an email: **Jim@happyhomeownerbook.com** and let's get started.

About the Author

As America's leading authority on the subject of Happy Homeownership, Jim has helped thousands of families preserve their dreams through every season of life. Jim has been working in the residential real estate business for more than 30 years. First, as a licensed real estate agent and rental property owner and for more than 10 years as a licensed insurance professional. Jim's knowledge of the residential real estate market, combined with his experience as a licensed insurance professional, makes him uniquely qualified to assist homeowners with lifetime home ownership.

Jim and his wife, Adriana, reside in Vestal, New York. They enjoy travelling to visit their grandchildren in Brooklyn and Connecticut. They also enjoy travelling around the world, including frequent trips to Adriana's native Colombia to visit friends and family.

Education

Broome Community College, AAS Business Administration

Binghamton University School of Management, BS Management Science

Kaplan Institute, Series 6 and 63 Securities Registered Representative

The American College, Chartered Life Underwriter

The American College, Chartered Financial Consultant

Languages

English, Spanish and Portuguese

Affiliations

Financial Planning Association

National Association of Insurance and Financial Advisors

Binghamton University Alumni Association

Greater Binghamton Association of Realtors

Greater Binghamton Chamber of Commerce

Made in the USA
Middletown, DE
20 December 2018